Do Your Ears Hang Low?

This is for Mr. Jeffries of West Sussex, England:
the basset hound with the world's largest ears!
They really DO hang low, according to the
Guinness Book of World Records 2004!

—J.U.

ISBN 0-439-73353-7

Text copyright © 2005 by Scholastic Inc.
Illustrations copyright © 2005 by Jackie Urbanovic.
All rights reserved. Published by Scholastic Inc.
SCHOLASTIC, SING AND READ STORYBOOK, and associated logos
are trademarks and/or registered trademarks of Scholastic Inc.

12 11 10 9 8 7 6 5 4 3 2   5 6 7 8 9 10/0

Printed in the U.S.A.
First printing, March 2005

Book design by Janet Kusmierski

Do Your Ears Hang Low?

Adapted by Rachel Lisberg
Illustrated by Jackie Urbanovic

SCHOLASTIC INC.
New York Toronto London Auckland Sydney
Mexico City New Delhi Hong Kong Buenos Aires

Do your ears hang low?
Do they wobble to and fro?

Can you tie them in a knot?
Can you tie them in a bow?

Can you throw them
over your shoulder
like a Continental
Soldier?

Do your ears hang low?

Do your ears hang high?
Do they reach up
to the sky?

Do they wrinkle when they're wet?
Do they straighten when they're dry?

Can you wave them at your teacher
every morning when you see her?

Do your ears hang high?

Do your ears hang wide?
Do they flap from side to side?

Do they wave in the breeze
from the slightest little sneeze?

Can you fly above your school?
All your friends will think you're cool!

Do your ears hang wide?

Do your ears hang low?
Do they wobble to and fro?
Can you tie them in a knot?
Can you tie them in a bow?

Can you throw them over your shoulder
like a Continental Soldier?
Do your ears hang low?

Do Your Ears Hang Low?

Do your ears hang low? Do they wob - ble to and fro? Can you

tie them in a knot? Can you tie them in a bow? Can you throw them o' - er your should-er like a

Con - ti - nen - tal sold-ier? Do your ears hang low?